WITHDRAWN

The Angel of Eleventh Avenue

ROY BATES

SOURCEBOOKS, INC.
NAPERVILLE, ILLINOIS

Published by Sourcebooks, Inc.
P.O. Box 4410, Naperville, Illinois 60567-4410
(630) 961-3900
FAX: (630) 961-2168
www.sourcebooks.com

Library of Congress Cataloging-in-Publication Data

Bates, Roy (LeRoy J.)
  The angel of Eleventh Avenue / By Roy Bates.
    p. cm.
  ISBN 1-40220-028-5 (Hardcover)
  1. Cancer—Patients—Fiction. 2. Cancer in children—Fiction.
  3. Mothers and daughters—Fiction. 4. Angels—Fiction.   I.
Title.
  PS3602.A87A54 2002
  813'.6—dc21
2002008767

Printed and bound in the United States of America
QW 10 9 8 7 6 5 4 3 2 1

A very special thank you to the artist
Simon Dewey
for the beautiful original painting on the cover,
and to Tim Leavitt, his agent,
both of whom contributed with heartfelt enthusiasm
to the entire project.

Also, my appreciation to Lisa May for her encouragement,
and New York Times *bestselling author,*
Richard Paul Evans for his kind endorsement.

ℬ

To the Angels...

The staff of Primary Children's Medical Center,
both past and present

The executive board and committee members
of the Festival of Trees,
and Cindy Knudsen,
who introduced us to the festival

Sharon Goodrich,
whose knowledge, experience, and insights
were invaluable

And the thousands of children,
and their loved ones,
who make up the entire Primary Children's Family

ℬ

Contents

Preface

It was thirty-eight years ago this spring that I first became acquainted with Primary Children's Hospital, and this story is my attempt to pay tribute to those wonderful spirits who have become such a special part of my memories. It is a very personal and sacred story to me, and one that encompasses all that I have imagined this place to be about.

The main characters are fictional, but the historical and geographical references are as accurate as I could make them.

The more familiar with children's hospitals that we become, the more we begin to understand that the actual stories of those who have become part of the histories of these magical places are far more miraculous than I, or anyone else, could ever capture in a book.

I hope you enjoy reading this, and may you be inspired to give of your heart freely to children everywhere.

—Roy Bates
August 2001

The Children's Hospital

Late at night when all is dark,
And the halls have all gone quiet and still,
When all the little aching bodies
Have finally found their sleep,

When a father's prayers have all been uttered,
And a mother's desperate pleas have all been made,
The night nurse sometimes hears a whisper
And smiles as she feels the warmth it brings.

It's then the heavens open up their gates,
And angels walk these sacred corridors.
A gentle unseen touch, a soft unspoken word,
A tender caress from beyond our reach.

It's true that God has a favorite place on earth,
Where the hosts of heaven intermingle,
And faith in the goodness of all mankind,
Radiates from every station.

This is His house, just a little south of heaven,
And these are his children, as noble as the angels.
And we who serve them are the lucky ones,
Blessed to share them both.

CHAPTER ONE

The

Festival

As the familiar melody reached her ears, Katherine Wilson caught her breath, and a warm tear rolled slowly down her cold cheek. At that same instant a stray breeze from the foyer of the Salt Palace sent a cool shiver across the back of her neck, prompting her to adjust the knitted scarf she was wearing. She touched Beverly's hand on the grips of her wheelchair to signal her to pause for a moment, and then she strained to listen.

On the small stage just ahead of them and beyond the gift shop, a solo woman's voice, sounding almost angelic, was singing:

And for me some scarlet ribbons
Scarlet ribbons for my hair…

Tears immediately began to flow freely, and as the song continued in the background, Katherine turned slightly and in a sobbing whisper said, "Thank you so much for bringing me here, Beverly. You don't know how much this means to me."

Since its beginning thirty years earlier, Katherine had never missed an opening night at the Festival of Trees. Having served on the executive board and several different committees for over twenty-five years, the festival had become as much a part of the season for her as the holidays themselves. This year was different, though. It was much, much different.

In August, after suffering for several months with ever-increasing pain, which she tried at first to dismiss as just part of aging, she had finally been convinced to seek medical advice. Then, following weeks of tests at the Huntsman Cancer Institute, the doctors had informed her that she had cancer. According to the diagnosis, it had started in her pancreas and had spread so far by the time it was discovered that neither a cure nor extended remission were realistic hopes.

The day she was told of the prognosis, her oncologist, Dr. Thomas Madison, had been sensitive but very matter-of-fact, "Of course you could get another opinion, Katherine. I know several other very good specialists I could refer you to."

She interrupted him, stammering, "And you're absolutely sure of the diagnosis? How long do I have?"

"Three, maybe four months. Five if we're lucky."

As he spoke, she just looked straight ahead blankly and then asked, "What have the other doctors said?"

"Katherine, I'm not going to give you any false hope. I've known you much too long, and I know you would see right through it anyway. I've consulted with everyone else here at the Center, and I'm afraid we all feel the same way."

He reached out and took her hand, and she gazed down at the floor for a moment. Then looking back up to him, she smiled weakly and announced, "Well, then, that's that I suppose. I guess I'm just going to have to do some getting ready, that's all."

Trying to find something to say, which always seemed impossible at such times, Dr. Madison offered, "I can have my secretary arrange for hospice services if you'd like."

She patted his hand and replied softly, "Maybe, but we'll see. We'll see."

It was strange, she thought at the time. She had always assumed that if news of this sort were ever presented to her that it would be devastating, but it was quite the opposite. At first she thought that maybe she was in denial, because it really didn't seem to bother her the way she thought it should. However, from the moment she received the news, an overwhelming sense of peace settled over her and seemed to follow her everywhere, and she had an unmistakably warm feeling inside that there was a wonderful reunion awaiting her soon.

Just then Kathy Winger and Helen Jones caught sight of Katherine, and after setting their clipboards on the table next to the gift shop, came to her and gave her a strong but gentle hug.

"Oh, we're so glad you could make it. Opening night wouldn't be the same without you," Kathy gushed. Smiling warmly, Helen echoed what Kathy had said, as Linda Marchant, who was still issuing instructions to someone on her walkie-talkie, joined them.

Kathy was the current chair of the festival, and Helen and Linda were serving as co-chairs. Together, they were responsible for supervising the work of over eighty members of the executive board, and nearly a thousand committee members. As was the case with all of the ladies who had been on the board for more than a couple of years, they were also dear friends.

Katherine turned to Linda and asked quietly, "Who was that group that just finished singing? I love that song."

At the same time that she was asking her question, the four ladies who had been singing were making their way to the exit down the next aisle twenty feet to their right. As they passed, the woman who had sung the solo turned momentarily and looked toward them.

For a moment the woman looked directly into Katherine's eyes. She looks so familiar, Katherine thought. Even from that distance it appeared as though the woman was trying desperately to keep her emotions in check.

Then, as if she had just realized that she had been discovered, she quickly gathered herself, smiled warmly at Katherine, and with a nod moved quickly out the door.

"I think they said they were the Sugar House Quartet," Linda replied. "I have seen the one who sang the solo around the hospital from time to time, but I don't really know any of their names. I'm sure this is their first year singing at the festival."

Katherine coughed slightly and confessed, "That song they were singing as we came in, 'Scarlet Ribbons,' is my favorite song in the whole world."

She paused a moment, and then looking up at her friends said, "I know it sounds odd to you ladies, but it seemed like they were singing that song just for my benefit."

Beverly bent toward Katherine and whispered, "If heaven has anything to say about who performs here and what they sing, then I'm sure they were."

Katherine squeezed her hand tightly and smiled as she said softly, "Thank you."

Beverly Freeman was the type of woman who everyone should have for a friend. With a personality as warm and inviting as a receiving blanket, it was no wonder that Katherine had liked her from the moment they had met. Years before, Katherine had taken Beverly under her wing when Beverly was new on the board, and though Katherine was old enough to be her mother, the two had become just like sisters.

Beverly's family had become like Katherine's own as well, and she knew that aside from her sister, Dorothy, it was Beverly and her family, more than anyone else in the world, to whom she most hated to say good-bye.

As each of the women on the board, together with their committee members, retreated to the aisles to assist those who were bidding on the trees, Beverly pushed Katherine's wheelchair carefully up and down each of the rows.

They stopped briefly to admire each individual tree, and as they did, it seemed to Katherine that there were more Tribute Trees this particular year than in the past. But of course, she thought, in her condition she was probably looking for them more this year than she ever had before.

℘

Each year, hundreds of trees are decorated, donated, and sold in an auction with all of the proceeds going to the hospital. These funds help ensure that no child, regardless of his or her circumstance, would ever be denied proper medical attention. In addition, each year several trees are decorated and donated in memory of a loved one. Over the years, this tradition of Tribute Trees has not only benefited the festival and the hospital greatly, but has also become a wonderful part of the healing process for those who have lost loved ones.

❦

It really is like magic, Katherine thought to herself, how everything connected with the festival benefits so many people, and how the community comes together in so many ways to make it happen.

At the end of the row of large trees on aisle M, they stopped to read the note the decorator had attached to the display. The arrangement took up both sides of the entire end of the row, and was titled *The Angel Garden*. As Katherine began to read, every emotion within her seemed to rise to the surface.

Last year, as my sister and I walked through the rows of beautiful trees, we commented to each other that though we have been here ten years and decorated ten different trees, we have never had the heart-wrenching task of doing a Tribute Tree. We felt very lucky.

Then, this past June, that same dear sister was diagnosed with cancer, and died shortly thereafter.

So this tree is lovingly dedicated to her and to this great festival that has served to bring us together in service to the children of the hospital, and to all that Primary Children's stands for.

Katherine brushed the tears from her eyes and, trying to sound light-hearted, blurted, "I'm just a blubbering old fool, Beverly. I guess I'm going to be an emotional basket case all evening. I hope you'll forgive me."

"I think that one gets to all of us," Beverly replied as she pushed Katherine's chair toward the rows of small table-top trees.

Just as they turned, out of the corner of her eye Katherine thought she noticed the woman from the singing group again. The lady was busy writing on a bid card at the end of the aisle near the exit. She looked up, seemed to catch Katherine's eye as if by accident, and quickly turned away.

"I thought they had left," Katherine said to herself, and then she turned to Beverly. "Do you think we could talk to that woman?" she asked her excitedly. "I would like to tell her how much I enjoyed her singing."

But no sooner had she made her request and turned back than she noticed the lady was nowhere to be seen. "Well, maybe if we see her again," she thought out loud.

They continued down that row past the small trees until they came to the one on the end where the woman had written the bid. It was a breathtakingly beautiful little tree, full from top to bottom, and decorated with deep red velvet bows and golden handmade ornaments.

On top of the tree was a gold-colored angel. Like many of the trees, this one had packages, all perfectly wrapped, arranged under its boughs for effect. The title on the display card simply read *Scarlet Ribbons*.

Katherine lowered her head, sobbing. Then, as she raised it up again, she just gazed straight ahead, as if she were looking at something either far away or from a long time ago. After several moments she took a deep breath, shook her head, and then once again reached up and gripped Beverly's hand tightly as if to make sure she was still there.

As the bidding deadlines moved from one group of rows to the next, Beverly and Katherine made their way to the main stage on the far side of the hall where the official lighting ceremony was to be held.

As they neared the stage, Beverly nudged Katherine on the shoulder, and motioned for her to turn to her right.

"How are you?" Katherine exclaimed as she recognized Kent McDonald. She looked up at him as she gripped his hand firmly.

"I'm doing well, thank you," he replied, then asked sincerely, "and how are you feeling, Katherine?"

"Actually I'm feeling better than I have in weeks," she answered honestly. Kent had not only been a great supporter of the hospital and the festival for years, but through their work together he had become a good friend as well.

As Katherine greeted Senator Wayne Skinner and the other dignitaries making their way to their seats, she marveled to herself at how free of pretense the atmosphere at the festival always seemed to be. Each year the highest of those on the social and economic ladder along with the most common in the city worked side by side as friends. Other than taking a sincere interest in each other's families, there didn't seem to be anything that mattered to them but their common objective.

Beverly smiled and gave her hand a good squeeze as she left Katherine and followed the others to the stand where she took her seat along with all of the past chairwomen of the festival. Katherine looked lovingly at the group of ladies sitting in that row, and smiled. What a magnificent group of women, she thought to herself. I shudder to think what my life would have been like without them.

As the guest celebrity, basketball star Jeff Hornacek was perfect for the part. Quiet and unassuming as always, he kept his remarks short, paying heartfelt tribute to the young people from the hospital with whom he shared the stage.

After a few minutes he turned the microphone over to Natalie Burdick, a young lady who had been a patient at the hospital frequently, and whom everyone close to the hospital knew very well.

As Natalie began her remarks, Katherine looked at the faces of those in the audience around her. Everyone was in awe of the twelve-year-old girl, who was speaking with the poise and depth of understanding of someone twice her age. As Natalie finished, Katherine smiled to herself and under her breath whispered, "Thank you, Beth."

If anyone had heard Katherine they couldn't have had any idea what she was talking about. But as she sat listening, an idea had begun to take shape within her. The more she went over it in her mind, the more powerful the desire became. She knew she had to tell them now. For years she had thought she should tell her story to Beverly and the others, but the right situation had never seemed to present itself.

This might be my last chance, she thought. This might be the last chance I'll ever have to share with my friends and pass on the gift I was given so many Christmases ago.

She looked up as Jeff and Natalie put their hands together and pulled the lever to turn on the lights that would officially kick off the 2000 Festival of Trees. At that moment a light went on inside her soul, and she knew that she was ready.

After Beverly had found her way back to Katherine's wheelchair and the crowd had begun to drift away, Katherine turned to her excitedly and asked, "Do you mind if we go back to the boardroom with the ladies rather than going home immediately? I have something I really need to tell you all, and I know if I don't tell you tonight, I might never get it told."

"Of course not," Beverly replied. "This is your night, and you are welcome to stay as long as you like."

Together they made their way toward the exit, and as they neared the door they both looked over to the table where those who had purchased trees were making their payments. Once again, Katherine caught a glimpse of the woman who had sung so beautifully earlier. The lady paused, looked toward her, smiled warmly, and then quickly made her way out the exit door on the south.

Katherine was thinking halfway out loud and was oblivious of anyone around her, "That woman had such a sweet voice," she muttered as she looked after her.

In the boardroom, Emily Thompson, the hospital liaison and another of Katherine's longtime friends, had just come in and was standing near the sofa. "I'm glad you are here, Emily," Katherine said. "I think I want you to hear what I have to say as much as, and maybe more than, anyone else."

As soon as Kathy, Helen, and Linda had come in and were seated, Beverly sat down next to Emily.

Katherine then began quietly, almost timidly. "Ladies, you all know how much you mean to me. I owe each of you more than I will ever be able to repay. Because of that, there is something very personal and sacred to me that I must share with you tonight, if you will allow me."

There was a kind of obedient reverence among the ladies as she asked them to stay and listen. Every one of them had come to love this dear sweet woman almost as a mother, and they all knew too well that this would, without question, be her last festival with them. So after a brief look and a nod to each other, they turned their attention to Katherine.

"This is a story I have never told anyone," she began. "And though he obviously knew some of it, not even my dear late husband knew it completely. After I finish, you may think I'm crazy, but as sure as I live, what I am going to tell you actually happened."

She turned to the two on her left and said, "Beverly and Emily, you were both here thirteen or fourteen years ago when that beautiful little girl from Midway spoke to us at our kickoff luncheon. I can't remember her name off the top of my head, but she was the one who had been hurt so badly in the car accident near the summit by Park City. Do you remember how she talked about the angels who waited on her during her recovery?"

Beverly was nodding as Emily spoke. "I remember her very well," she said. "I think she touched everybody's heart that day."

Katherine smiled, then nodded and continued. "As you listened to her, did you get the impression that she was talking about actual angels, or just others from the hospital?"

Beverly answered sincerely, "I guess I never tried to analyze it one way or another. Is it important?"

"In one respect I suppose that it probably isn't that important," Katherine replied. "But the thing I'm getting at is that we talk about angels all of the time as we deal with the festival and the hospital, but have any of you ladies actually seen one?"

She looked at each of the women in the group as they looked at each other. Nothing was said for the longest time, and then Katherine herself broke the silence.

She lowered her head briefly, took a deep breath, and looking directly at them, said simply, "Well, I have."

Each of their eyes grew wide, and they all leaned forward as she continued. "The story I want to tell you is about one very special angel I met a long time ago. This story began nearly fifty years ago, long before the Festival of Trees, and as far as I am concerned, in another lifetime."

CHAPTER TWO

The Ones We Love

To give you the proper background I guess I should go back to when Dan and I met. Some of you ladies may have known my husband. Beverly and Emily, I know you both did. Well, we met while we were attending the University, and I fell in love with him immediately. He was a tall, handsome graduate student with an engineering degree, and I was just finishing my sophomore year. I quickly made up my mind that no matter what it took, I was going to convince him to fall in love with me. Whatever I did, it must have worked because we were married two years later, in April of 1951, just two weeks before graduation.

Like most newly married couples, we thought we had the world on a string, and as far as we were concerned, nothing could go wrong. Dan had finished his master's degree, and I had my teaching certificate and was ready to go.

Right away we put a down payment on a pretty little two-bedroom home on Bryan Avenue. It was only a few blocks from Liberty Park and just down the street from Whittier Elementary, where I had been offered a job teaching third grade. Dan had had interviews with the engineering departments of several companies, and we felt confident that at least one of them would offer him a position.

We really should have expected what was to come next I suppose. The Korean War was going on, and Dan's school deferment had just expired, so it should not have come as a surprise. But nonetheless it did.

On the morning of the sixth of June, we received that fateful letter many feared. It was Dan's draft notice telling us that he was to report by the first of August for basic training. I remember that I was in the kitchen when he opened the letter, and when he handed it to me, I just froze.

"What are we going to do?" I cried. "This isn't fair, it just isn't fair."

He just sighed and held me tightly in his arms. "I guess the army needs engineers, too. At least I will go in as an officer; that's a plus, I suppose."

I remember thinking to myself how angry I was at him for taking it so calmly. I know I wasn't really angry at him, only the circumstances we found ourselves in. It's just that it seems so much easier to direct those kinds of emotions at someone close and tangible.

Then came another big surprise. Though preparing for him to leave would have been hard enough by itself, three weeks before he was to report, our doctor told us that we were going to have a baby.

I remember thinking to myself at the time, This is all I need; what else is going to go wrong now?

We had a very short time together following his basic training, time I more or less wasted feeling sorry for myself. Then he shipped out for Korea, and I found myself alone. I was very discouraged and negative about everything in my life. Here I am, I thought, a newlywed mother-to-be, halfway through a pregnancy, a rookie teacher with all of the challenges that come with that, and my husband has just left me. Never mind that he had no choice and would have given anything to be home with me.

For so many years following that period I hated myself for my actions then, but all I could think about at the time was how inconvenient this baby was making things. I was always sick, which didn't help my attitude at all. I knew I was a terrible teacher, and by Thanksgiving, I was at the end of my rope.

In today's world we are quite a bit more educated and sympathetic about the depression that sometimes accompanies pregnancy, but in 1951 a woman in my situation was pretty much on her own.

To complicate matters, the letters from Dan, rather than helping my attitude, just seemed to infuriate me more. He wasn't there to help, I thought to myself, and I cursed him for it. He was far away playing soldier. Of course the thought of having a child was wonderful to him; he wasn't having it.

Angry, alone, bitter, and feeling as low as I had ever felt in my life, I wrote a letter to Dan that would have destroyed the strongest of men. In that letter I blamed him for everything. I told him that our marriage was a mistake, that I had never loved him, and how I didn't want any part of his baby. I have done some pretty stupid things in my life, but I think that still remains the meanest and most shameful thing I have ever done.

I quit my teaching job just before Christmas, and my younger sister, Dorothy, came to be with me until the baby was born. Having her there helped a great deal, and slowly over the next four weeks my spirits improved. It really seemed to help to have someone to talk to.

In the letter I received from Dan in January he said nothing about the Christmas letter I had sent, but I did notice that his letter was less personal and more matter-of-fact than his previous ones had been.

The truth of the matter was that as my due date drew closer, I began to look forward more and more to becoming a mother. Somehow that little life inside of me was taking hold of my heart and attaching itself to my soul like nothing I had ever experienced. And feeling much better, I seemed to be able to put what I had said to Dan aside in a corner of my mind and not think about it. I think I had also succeeded in convincing myself that he had been able to do the same thing as well.

Then came that awful night. I awoke around two A.M. with intense pains and bleeding. Knowing deep inside that something was terribly wrong, I asked Dorothy to drive me to the hospital. We arrived there at 2:45, and that was the last thing I remembered until late in the afternoon.

When the doctor came to my room I knew it was bad news before he even spoke. With his head lowered, not wanting to look me in the eye, and with his voice cracking, he announced that after eight and a half months of pregnancy, my baby boy had been stillborn.

I was numb. In fact I was more than numb; I was dead. There were things going on all around me—my sister was there and the nurses were there, but none of them could penetrate where I was emotionally. The only thought I had was that I had deserved it, and that God was punishing me. My attitude and my selfishness had cost me my baby.

I remembered immediately every vicious word I had written to Dan. I remembered them over and over again, and when I went to sleep I remembered them in my dreams. I was going to lose my husband as well; I knew it. In fact I felt as though I had to, as though even trying to keep him would mean that I was not willing to accept what I was sure I deserved.

Then I did another very foolish thing. Rather than pouring out my heart and telling Dan how badly I felt and how much I was hurting inside, which is what I should have done, I wrote him a letter that was coolly to the point and matter of fact:

> *Dear Dan,*
>
> *Two days ago, February 2nd, we had a stillborn son. I am very sorry. I know what you must think of me right now. I'm sure you will probably not want to write to me again after what I said before, and I don't blame you. It's probably for the best anyway.*
>
> > *Sincerely,*
> > *Katherine*

It seemed as though, given where my thoughts were coming from at the time, that was all I was worthy to say; but I soon realized that if my first letter had broken his heart, this one had put a dagger through it. What on earth was I thinking? I had married the finest man I had ever met, and within six months of him being gone from me, I had at first convinced myself that he was a demon, and then later that I was.

It's sad how things happen sometimes, but the events of those months were to haunt me for the next fourteen years.

For the time being, though, it seemed like it was easier to cope with all of the guilt I felt, along with the intense pain of losing a child, by burying it deep inside myself in a place where I wouldn't have to deal with it. It was a time when I should have been seeking help from the Lord, but I didn't. Besides, I had convinced myself that after what I had done, if there was a God as I had been taught, then He would want nothing to do with me.

CHAPTER THREE

Becky

$\mathcal{S}$pring came early, and the apricots had already blossomed before I heard again from Dan. When I did, it was due in a large part to the efforts of a busybody little sister. While I was bent on emotional self-destruction, she had taken the time in the weeks following my loss to write him a sympathetic and detailed account of all that had happened. At the same time, she assured him in the strongest way she knew how that I was still in love with him.

The letter I received from him early that spring was beautiful and is still with me today. I cried all night as I read and reread his tender words. He apologized over and over again that he had not been able to be there to help me when I needed him. He also told me that he had had a dream the night our son was born. He didn't tell me what the dream was, but he said it made him feel at peace and helped him to understand that everything would be all right.

He finished his letter with another plea for forgiveness and wrote:

For better or for worse, for richer or for poorer, in sickness and in health, whatever the case might be, I will always love you.

Your devoted husband,
Dan

Even though that letter didn't erase the guilt I felt within myself, at least I was sure that I would have a chance to make it up to him in some way.

I was able to complete the entire school year of 1952–53, and being involved teaching my students was wonderful therapy. Dan and I wrote to each other constantly, and our letters became almost as intimate as they had been in the beginning. Still, I knew there were things that needed to be said that could only be said face to face and wounds that could only be healed in person. In our letters we never spoke at all about the pregnancy, either. I guess it was too painful for both of us.

During the summer of '53 I received a letter nearly every day, and by the time I got the notice telling me that he would be home on the 15th of September, I was fit to be tied. My students were excited for me as well, and they all helped me make little gifts and signs to welcome him home.

I want to say that when we saw each other at the train station, it was just like it had been before, but it wasn't. When he had left we were just kids, but by the time he returned home, it seemed like I had a soul mate.

It's strange how much easier it is to say some things in a letter than it is in person, and how much deeper some thoughts can go when two people are apart. Through his letters, I had developed an appreciation that the man I greeted that day at the train station had become a much deeper, more spiritual man than the one I had married.

We said very little to each other during the ten-minute ride from the depot to our home. We just kept glancing at each other nervously, and he kept squeezing my hand in his.

I remember how nice it was to sit in the passenger side for a change, and how proud I was to be sitting next to him. As we turned off Third East down Bryan Avenue and pulled into our driveway, my heart was beating so wildly that I can almost still feel it today.

Together we climbed the steps of the wooden porch, and he opened the door for me before hauling his huge duffle into the entryway. I was standing in the archway between the kitchen and the entry when he turned to face me, and I looked up into those eyes that had so captivated me nearly four years earlier. There was no hesitation there, no judgment, nothing but love.

I started to say something and had to catch myself. I bit my lower lip to keep it from quivering and started to speak again, and then I lost it. I completely collapsed into his arms, sobbing uncontrollably. He led me to the sofa, sat me down with my head in his arms, and gently pushed my hair back away from my face. That evening I cried in his arms until every tear I had stored up for so long had completely soaked his dress uniform.

The days following were good days for us. Dan quickly found work, and we began to enjoy the carefree life of a young married couple. By then, I was feeling much more confident as a teacher. That, and the fact that we had survived the Army, gave us the feeling that we could get through almost anything.

Though we really should have done so, I don't ever remember sitting down with him and talking through all of those things that I was so sure needed to be talked through. It was as though we both preferred to think that the early part of our life was safely in the past, locked up in a trunk somewhere where it couldn't hurt either of us.

In March of '54 I received the news I had hoped for since Dan returned home, and in September I gave birth to our beautiful little Rebecca. Finally I had someone to share the love that I felt should have belonged to our son.

From the time she was born, I did exactly that. Every thing I could give her I did. If she showed a desire to take dance lessons, she took them. If she wanted to learn the piano, I found the best teacher available. And when she showed an interest in the violin, I drove her to Farmington every week for over three years, so that she could be taught by the best.

With all we gave her she certainly could have been a spoiled child, but she was just the opposite. She was naturally kind and gentle and seemed to be completely without any selfishness or malice. I often wondered to myself back then why such an angelic child should be placed in my care. I thought I was as out of harmony with God as a person could be. I never had any interest at all in attending church or participating actively with those who did. I had no particular use for religion, and could not bring myself to think that a prayer to God had any real meaning.

Still, in my heart I was happy that Dan and Becky did. She would get up on Sunday morning every week and ask, "Do you want to go to Sunday School with us today, Mamma?"

And every week my answer would be about the same: "Oh, I've got too many papers to grade, but you can tell me all about it when you get home."

One thing we discovered after Becky was born was that she was to be our last child. When the doctor gave us that news, I remember that it meant very little to me at the time, and I don't remember ever being baby-hungry as Becky was growing up. I had my child; that was all I needed. Besides, I was certain there was only enough room in my heart for one child at a time. How very little I knew about love and children and sacrifice, and the blessings that accompany them.

As you can imagine, with that narrow perspective I was as unprepared for the turn of events in our life as a person could have been.

CHAPTER FOUR

Strength
and
Weakness

The Holidays in 1965 were the best I could ever remember. On Christmas Eve, the three of us took a drive in the car down State Street from the capitol building to Midvale. We stopped first for few minutes to admire the sparkling lights and then to look at the window displays in the stores downtown. Then, after stopping briefly at my sister's house, we came back to 21st South and took our traditional route past the beautiful stores in Sugar House. I have always loved Sugar House, especially at Christmas, and Dan and Becky felt like no day was truly wonderful unless it included a stop at Snelgrove's for ice cream.

A light snow began falling just as we drove up to the house that evening, and it continued steadily through Christmas morning. I remember that as Dan and I sat together, watching Becky open her gifts, with the snow falling lightly outside the front room window, it felt almost like we were part of a picture on a Christmas card.

At that moment neither of us could have ever dreamed how dramatically our lives would change before we would see another Christmas together, and how different that Christmas would be.

It was only a short time after the holidays that we began to see a change in Becky. Dan and I had both noticed that since just after Christmas she had become increasingly listless in her behavior. Though normally full of energy and enthusiasm, she was getting tired way too easily and seemed to lack all interest in those things she most liked to do. Until then, I had never seen a time when she would rather sleep during the middle of the day than play.

Becky had an accident while sledding with her friends the day before Christmas that year, and though her scrapes seemed minor and didn't concern us much at the time, as the days passed, they just didn't seem to heal.

After observing these things for three or four weeks, we really didn't know what to do, and were beginning to become frightened.

Between the twenty-first of January and the seventh of February, we took her to see our family doctor three different times. At first he tried to assure us that it was business as usual, but we both could see that he was more than a little concerned. After ruling out a variety of things that she didn't have, he finally referred us to a specialist at St. Marks Hospital.

I remember very clearly that February of 1966 was a particularly cold and miserable month. For nearly three weeks, the entire valley had been covered with a suffocating layer of dense fog. During those inversions, which happened at least once each winter, it seemed that everyone's attitude just naturally got a little more negative. So, after two weeks of tests, even before we were told the news, I was already feeling the strain.

When the doctors finally told us that Becky had leukemia, I remember that I was sitting down, but I felt as though I had just been dropped out of an airplane without a parachute.

"This can't be happening, Dan," I sobbed, and I put my head on his shoulder. Right then, even more than when our son was born, I wished that my life would end.

Dan couldn't even speak. His eyes were fixed straight ahead, but I knew he wasn't looking at anything. Becky was his whole life. Oh, I know he loved me more than I was willing to admit, but I don't think there had ever been a father who had worshipped a daughter more than he did Becky

"You are God's little gift to our family," he would always tell her, "and He's just going to have to run heaven with one less angel for a while."

So as the doctor prescribed what little treatment was available, we just nodded and fought back the tears.

It was truly amazing, but right from the beginning Becky was by far the strongest of the three of us. It was as if she had just been presented a new hand of cards to play, and she immediately began the process of figuring out how best to play them. She didn't spend much time feeling sorry for herself, as I would have done, nor did she often ask why it was happening to her and not to other children.

All through the spring and summer she would go through the cycles of heavy symptoms, medication, and periods of relief. During all of this, her spirits couldn't have been better. Her attitude was always, "It's going to be all right, Mamma," but I was certain that she really didn't understand the seriousness of her condition.

It's much different now, but in 1966 the prognosis for a child suffering from leukemia was very bleak. It's only been in the last twenty-five years or so that the chemotherapy and bone marrow treatments have become effective enough to give any real hope to the families.

Our doctor had been very honest in his assessment from the beginning, and we knew there was very little real hope of recovery for our little girl.

Through it all, my attitude was by far the hardest thing for me to deal with. As the days grew into weeks and then months, I grew increasingly bitter. The unfairness of every-thing greeted me when I woke up in the morning, and I took the same feelings to bed with me at night.

It wasn't long before I had shut Dan completely out of my life as well. Somehow I had convinced myself that to love my daughter properly, I had to give her my full atten-tion, and the way I saw it, that left no room for any rela-tionship with anyone else. It still amazes me how twisted I had let my logic become, and how suffocating guilt and self-pity can be.

Dan was as patient as a person could be, I suppose, but I could tell the stress was getting to him, too. He was by nature a very positive individual, but the fatigue he was feeling seemed to be affecting his spirit and mind as well as his body.

Why I reacted so coldly on some things I can't really say, but during that time the one thing I totally refused to do with my little girl was pray. She had asked me several times if I would, and in what I thought was a loving way I would always say, "No, dear, but I will be here with you while you pray." As day after day she offered her soul to God I kept telling myself, "If it makes her feel a little better, then there is certainly no harm in it."

At the same time I was reinforcing within myself the feeling that it was a complete waste. If there was a God, and

I had really made the effort to convince myself that I didn't actually think there was, then I was not the sort of person He was going to remember anyway.

Not that my negative approach needed a boost, but what happened to Dan in August only seemed to fuel my attitude. He had always been so healthy and athletic that his heart attack came as a complete shock. He arrived home after work more tired than usual one afternoon and went straight to bed. He fell asleep immediately, but woke up a little while later gasping for breath. In typical understated fashion he simply came to the door of the kitchen and said calmly, "Honey, I think I need to get to a hospital."

Though I'm sure I didn't see it that way at the time, we were very fortunate that it was no worse than it was. As it turned out, the recovery period was relatively short as far as heart attacks go, but it did cause him to have to quit his job for a time. Because of that, among other things, we ended up losing our benefits.

His employer had always paid Dan's insurance, so we had never bothered to take the policy that was offered through the school district. Besides, with our daughter's condition growing progressively worse, I had already taken a leave of absence to be with her. So we ended up without any insurance, as well as without any income.

So that was the situation we found ourselves in: Becky needing more and more medical attention, both of us out of work, and our savings rapidly running out. As Dan and I looked at our deteriorating financial situation, we figured that by Thanksgiving we would be completely broke.

I can't tell you how desperate I felt. Everything that I had always counted on—our savings, our ability to work, our health—everything that provided us a sense of security had, in a matter of a few months, either been used up completely or was dwindling rapidly.

Still, as depressed and discouraged as I was, I refused to turn to God. That is exactly what I should have done, but I just couldn't. Dan, however, continued to pray regularly with Becky, and was always tolerant of my desire not to. Up until that time it hadn't bothered me much, but little by little I began to be jealous of that part of their relationship. Still, unless the God they were praying to had a bag of money to leave on my doorstep or some kind of miracle cure for our daughter, I felt like He was of no use to me.

Even when Dorothy tried to arrange for us to speak to the people at Primary Children's Hospital, I remained resolute and prideful in my attitude toward God. We wanted so desperately to be able to provide for her, but Becky's condition had deteriorated to the point that, by mid-November, we knew she would need extended hospitalization somewhere. So, reluctantly, with our pride severely bruised, our savings gone, and no insurance, we admitted her to Primary Children's.

They say in every life there is one point in time that has the potential to virtually define one's existence. If that's true, then being introduced to the Primary Children's Hospital was that point for me. It was there that, slowly and subtly at first and later quite dramatically, my life and my heart began to change.

CHAPTER FIVE

The Children's Hospital

It was just after dawn on the Monday morning before Thanksgiving in 1966 when we turned the car north on Fifth East and headed to the hospital. Becky had been so careful as we left the house to make sure that all of her things were in place and the curtains in her room were left open so the sun could shine in. As Dan picked her up in his arms to carry her to the car, she had him stop at the door for a minute so that she could turn back to look.

She seemed to be taking inventory of everything, cataloguing the contents so she could keep the images alive in her mind. She smiled weakly and almost prophetically asked, "I wonder if this is the last time I will see our home?"

I was so close to breaking down in tears that I couldn't face her as we walked to the car. Till then I had not permitted myself to even think in those terms, and there she was, so simply and matter-of-factly, stating what we all knew was most likely to happen. I admired her strength and the direct way she expressed herself, but I still couldn't help feeling that at twelve years of age, she didn't quite comprehend what was going on.

She arrived at the hospital with only a small suitcase that contained a few of her clothes and the candy box she kept her paper dolls in. We introduced ourselves at the desk, and immediately we were treated like honored guests.

I remember thinking, what a stark contrast. It was such a different feeling than we had experienced at the other hospitals we had been to.

Dan and I stayed back for a few minutes to fill out papers while one of the nurses escorted Becky to her room. They had assigned her to one on the fifth floor with a window that looked southwest over the valley.

A little while later, as we were sitting by her bedside, she commented, "These people are so nice to me, Mamma, I feel like a princess."

I smiled back at her while I adjusted her pillow, "That's because you are a princess, Dear."

She just grinned back at me, "I love you so much, Mamma." She looked at Dan sheepishly and a little guilty look came over her face. "Oh, and I love you, too, Daddy."

We both took her in our arms, and she almost giggled as she said, "We haven't had a three-way hug in a long time. I love three-way hugs."

Dan caught my eye and for a moment I thought of just throwing my arms around him and never letting go. I had kept him at arm's length for so long and had avoided looking too deeply into his eyes for fear of what I might find. Sadly for me, I was able to resist the impulse, and we both sat down in our chairs and began talking with Becky about other things.

I don't know what made me do the things I did sometimes, but what my heart wanted more than anything in the world was to be held and loved like I remembered. I knew in my heart that Dan felt the same way, that all he longed for was to take a break from all of the sadness and the despair, and just hold me. But I just couldn't let it happen.

As much as it hurt, and I know it hurt him at least as much as it did me, I could not let anything penetrate the shell I thought was all that was keeping me together.

$\mathcal{C}$

The members of the hospital staff were very kind and accommodating and made arrangements for us to spend Thanksgiving that year together in Becky's room. We had our dinner with all of the traditional trimmings: turkey, cranberry sauce, stuffing, pumpkin pie, and even a little carrot pudding that Dorothy and her family had made for us. It was wonderful.

For that entire afternoon we ate and played board games together. And even though Becky got tired very quickly, for a short time we almost forgot all about leukemia, medications, hospitals, doctors, and everything. It's funny how in that place, even though we were in a hospital, it almost didn't feel like one.

Twice that afternoon, other children from the same floor came to Becky's room to see her. The first was a little girl who was being treated for burns on both of her arms. She was so pretty the way she smiled when I asked her what she was there for.

You could tell she was hurting, but she forced a big smile. "Doctor Broadbent is going to take some of my skin from here," and she pointed to her hip, "and put it here," motioning to her arms.

"What a brave little girl," I said to her. And I meant every word of it.

About thirty minutes after her visit, while we were eating some pudding, a boy who looked to be about eight years old poked his head around the corner.

"That looks really good," he said hopefully.

Dan winked at Becky and responded, "Hi, slugger, what's your name?"

He wasn't the least bit timid. "David," he said proudly. "I'm Becky's friend, and that pudding looks really good."

Dan just chuckled and asked him, "Would you like to have some with us?" Then he picked the little boy up and sat him on the edge of Becky's bed. As I spooned out some pudding into a bowl for him, Dan asked, "So what are you here for, tiger?" We noticed that he had a bandage the size of a grapefruit covering his left hand.

"I got my hand caught in a machine, and the doctors are going to try to make some of my fingers work again," he said, more interested in getting a bite of pudding into his mouth than anything else.

I could tell Dan really liked that little guy as he kept asking him questions. "So, you are Becky's friend, are you?"

"Yep," he said as he kept eating. "She's really pretty, 'cept I think she's probably too old for me as a girlfriend or anything."

Dan just about split his sides trying not to laugh.

As they continued to talk and Becky watched in amusement, I just stared at Dan. I hadn't seen him laugh like that for what seemed an eternity, and I liked what I saw.

ଔ

I really cannot put an exact time on it because it happened so gradually, but as I watched the way the staff catered to our little girl, and how the other children in the hospital got along with each other, my heart began to soften.

There was something magical about that place. I hadn't been able to identify exactly what it was, but it felt very special.

I remember a time when Dan and I were driving up to see Becky one evening. The lawns were covered with a blanket of new snow, and the trees were especially beautiful, all covered in white and bending under the weight of the snow on their limbs. As we turned the car onto Eleventh Avenue and looked to the north, we could see the hospital sitting up on the hill above us.

The lights were on and the brightness of the moon on the snow made the entire scene seem to glow.

Speaking half to himself and half to me, Dan mused, "There is a part in the Bible when Jesus, speaking to his disciples, declares, 'Ye are the light of the world, a city that is upon a hill cannot be hid.' Katherine, in some ways I really believe he could have been talking about this place."

Surprised, I turned to him. "I didn't know you knew the Bible so well," I exclaimed.

"I know a lot of things better than I once did," he returned matter-of-factly and somewhat to himself.

CHAPTER SIX

Scarlet
Ribbons

$\mathcal{I}$ remember the first time we heard the song "Scarlet Ribbons" together. I was sitting with Becky in her hospital room on a Sunday afternoon, just three days after Thanksgiving. She had her little transistor radio on with the earphone in her ear, and I was reading a magazine. Suddenly, she took the earphone out and exclaimed, "Mamma, you have to hear this song. I heard it yesterday after you and Daddy left, and it's so beautiful."

She turned the radio up, and we listened to the Lennon Sisters as they blended their voices perfectly to form the melody. As the song ended, she turned to me excitedly, "Don't you just love that song, Mamma? I'll bet that little girl loved her mamma, just like I love you."

I really wasn't prepared for that. I quickly wiped a tear from my eye and replied, "And I'm sure her mother loved her just like I love you." I bent over and kissed her on the forehead and couldn't help but take a moment to look into her beautiful blue eyes.

I was still amazed at what I saw. Unlike mine, which if you were to have looked into them then you may have seen a dozen emotions, most of them dark, what I saw in hers was a sparkle that completely contradicted her condition. Her body may have been suffering, but the spirit that radiated through her eyes was as healthy as ever, maybe more so.

With an impish grin, she leaned over and pulled her box out from beneath her bed. Then she took out a small piece of paper, wrote something quickly on it and, putting it back in, slid the box back under her bed.

Of all the nice things she owned and had received from Christmases and birthdays past, that beat-up old candy box was her favorite. When we left home, we told her she could take three or four of her favorite things to the hospital, but that box and what was in it was all she wanted to take.

It was a simple white cardboard "See's Candies" box that we had emptied from the previous Christmas. I never did know what the attraction was, but she really liked it and wouldn't let us throw it away. During that year, many of her treasures had been stored in it at one time or another, but all she had in it when she went to the hospital were her paper dolls and a pencil and paper.

"What are you doing?" I asked, smiling.

"I just wanted to remind myself of something I wanted for Christmas," she replied.

I choked a little as I caught myself. The desire of my heart was that she would be here and able to enjoy at least this one last Christmas with us.

"Can I read what it is?" I inquired, thinking of our finances and being almost afraid to see.

She surprised me again when she said, "I'm going to ask God when I pray tonight if He thinks it would be all right for me to ask for it," and she winked at us as she continued, "and if it is, then I'll show you tomorrow."

What a difference a year can make, I thought at the time. Just the Christmas before we were celebrating as if our lives and good health would go on forever. I didn't think we had gone overboard, but we certainly felt we had bought ourselves everything we truly wanted. Dan had given me the most beautiful ruby necklace and earrings, and I had bought him a new recliner for his den. For the family, we had replaced our old phonograph with a new console hi-fi stereo and stocked it with several new record albums.

I still have this picture in my mind of Nat King Cole's Christmas album playing in the background, and the three of us sitting by the fire, eating and laughing and singing along with the record.

It's ironic how the pictures of those two very different Christmases are etched in my mind like a matching set. I have never been able to think about one without thoughts of the other immediately following.

That night we stayed with Becky until visiting hours ended at 8:00 P.M., and after hugs and kisses Dan and I rode the elevator down to the main level and headed for the door. We stopped for a moment to speak to one of the nurses we had become familiar with, and just as we were turning to go out the door, I remembered that I had left my purse in Becky's room.

"You wait for me here," I told Dan, "I'll run back up and get it."

"If you're going to do that," he suggested, "I'll pull the car around so I can pick you up at the door."

I hurried back to the elevator, and after waiting for a moment or two, I got on and watched as the light signaled the fourth floor and then the fifth. Making my way out of the elevator, I walked quickly down the hall and opened Becky's door.

I stopped abruptly as I noticed her. She was half sitting up, her head bowed with her eyes closed and her arms folded in front of her.

"Heavenly Father, thank you for my mamma and daddy, and thank you for this hospital, the people here are so good to me."

She hesitated briefly, and then, as if she had been thinking of something, said, "and Heavenly Father, I know that I am probably going to be seeing you soon, but..."

And she paused again.

When I heard those words, tears started to roll down my cheeks. I didn't dare make a sound that might disturb her, so I just held my breath and listened.

"I was wondering if you thought it would be all right to ask Mamma and Daddy for some ribbons like the little girl in the song. I know they don't have much money any more, they've had to spend all of it trying to make me better..."

I have never in my life, either before or after, been pierced through the heart like I was then.

I listened as she continued:

"...but more than that, Heavenly Father, what I really wanted to ask you is to please bless Mamma. I love her so much, and I know Daddy loves her more than anything in the world. Help her to understand that I really am okay. She is so sad all of the time. Please find some way to make her happy. Thank you for listening to me tonight, Heavenly Father, I'll talk to you again tomorrow. In the name of Jesus, Amen."

Shaking to the very core of my being, there was no way on earth I was going to walk in on her then. So, deciding to leave my purse there until the next day, I stumbled past the nurse's station, onto the elevator, out the front door, and collapsed in the front seat of the car.

CHAPTER SEVEN

An Early Christmas

For the following two and a half weeks, Becky's physical condition continued to deteriorate. During that time, I nearly lived at the hospital and left only when I needed to.

Back then the rules on visitations were much stricter than they are today, and parents were required to leave by a specific time every evening. If regulations had been what they are now, I'm sure I would have stayed there continuously.

By that time, Dan had been cleared to go back to work, and though it forced us to plan a little more carefully, it seemed to ease the pressure just a little to know that we would have at least some income. So, in order to have as much time as possible to spend with Becky, he arranged to work the night shift.

Most mornings we were able to go and see her together. Dan would then go home and sleep for a few hours and come back in time to spend some time with us in the evening before going to work. The time away from the hospital at work seemed to help his spirits some, but the arrangement left me alone at nights with nothing to keep me company but the stereo and the TV.

I had plenty of time during those days to reflect, and more than enough to reflect on as well. Since the night when I had overheard my daughter's prayer, my heart had been in turmoil, and it had become increasingly difficult for me to maintain the cynical, defensive position I had taken in relation to God. In spite of myself, I noticed deeper and more sublime thoughts struggling to take hold of my heart.

Though I successfully fought off the urge for a time, I kept feeling strongly compelled to pour out my soul to Him in prayer.

Each night, during the late evening, after I had returned from the hospital and Dan had left for work, I would slowly talk myself into feeling like God really was there and that I needed to speak to Him. Then, each time I felt as though I was almost ready, it was as if a dark curtain would come down over my soul. Desperate and negative thoughts would take over, and I would once again go to sleep feeling empty inside. Over and over I went through the same process, and it seemed like the conflict would never end.

One bright spot was that I was able to find some beautiful scarlet ribbons made out of velvet at a little Sprouse Reitz store I passed each day on the way to the hospital. I was so excited to find them, and anxious to have the chance to give them to Becky.

Carolyn, one of the nurses there who had become especially close to Becky, had suggested a few days before that we have an early Christmas for her. When we thought about her condition and how fast she was failing, Dan and I jumped at the idea.

We planned it together and on December 18th, just one week before Christmas, we had a delightful little holiday celebration for her in her room. Since Dan had not received his first check yet, we had almost no money, but he still managed to find a new set of paper dolls for her. Even though Becky was physically very weak, she was still visibly delighted as she opened her gifts.

She opened the ribbons and the paper dolls at the same time and then started to cry. "How did you know, Mamma? I forgot to tell you what I wanted."

"Mammas know a little more than you think they do sometimes," I said as I winked at her.

"And, Daddy, do you know who this paper doll is?"

The paper dolls Dan had gotten her were of Janet Lennon from the Lennon Sisters. It must have been the perfect gift because she informed us that Janet was the one who had sung the solo on the song she liked so much.

She held the ribbons up against her cheek and touched the paper doll and then put her arms around me. She hugged me as tightly as her sick little body would let her and whispered in my ear, "I love you, Mamma." She looked at Dan and smiled, "And, Daddy, thank you so much. The paper dolls are perfect."

"Wait just a minute," Carolyn interrupted, "We're not through yet," and she signaled to the other nurse who was standing next to her.

I guess the nurses knew more about Becky than I had thought because they handed her a little flat present that was about six or seven inches square. She opened it slowly, and a tear rolled down her cheek as she looked first at Carolyn and then at me. What she found was a 45-rpm record of the song "Scarlet Ribbons."

She held it up close to her and sighed until one of the nurses who had left the room a moment earlier came back in, announcing, "Let's play it." She carried a little blue leatherette phonograph over to the table by the window and plugged it in.

The words to the song were so beautiful. Together we all listened to the sweet harmony, and every eye was on Becky as she just leaned back against her pillow, closed her eyes, and smiled.

Dan had to be at work earlier than usual that evening, so I drove him across town, and then came back to spend the last couple of hours of visiting time with Becky.

She was more awake and alert than she had been in days, and after a few minutes of talking about nothing in particular she turned to me and asked, "How are you doing, Mamma? Are you feeling any better?"

That was the first time she had asked me anything like that directly. "Oh, Honey, I'm doing just fine," I insisted. "I'm just worried about you and how you're doing." I bent down and brushed my hand against her cheek and kissed her gently.

She looked into my eyes and very seriously and sincerely announced: "Mamma, you don't need to worry about me. I have angels that stay here with me when you're gone, and they are very good to me."

My eyes grew to twice their usual size, and I gasped, "You what?" I really didn't know what to say.

"Yes, Mamma, they come every night. Sometimes they even listen to the radio with me. There are three or four of them that I have seen, but mostly it's just one. Her name is Beth, and she's been so nice. I think she likes my song, too. She said she did, and she knows everything about the hospital."

I was completely taken aback. Of all the fantastic ideas. There are no such thing as angels, I thought to myself. Then suddenly I heard a woman's voice behind me ask softly, "Why not, Katherine?"

I turned around quickly, but there was nobody there.

Before I left for home I watched as Becky pulled out her box, took out the paper dolls that were in it, and replaced them with the Janet Lennon paper doll. On top of the paper doll and its clothes she put her new record and the ribbons I had given her.

As I stood to leave and leaned down, she put her arms around my neck and said, "Mamma, I know this isn't the exact day, but I think that this is my favorite Christmas ever."

Like I had done so many times before, I cried all the way home.

ß

Day by day from then on her condition continued to fail rapidly. More and more of the time I had with her was spent sitting by her bedside reading magazines and thinking. I would sit and look at her as she slept and all of a sudden, out of nowhere, I would just break down crying. Though at the time it seemed like the days passed by so slowly, as I look back on that week now, everything just runs together as one brief, dark, cloudy period of time.

When she was awake for short periods Becky was very weak but as pleasant as ever. I would ask her each time she awoke, "How are you feeling, Sweetheart?"

And each time she would smile weakly and reply, "I'm doing okay, Mamma. The angels are teaching me lots of things, and they are really nice to me."

On Christmas Eve, Becky was sleeping soundly and the room was quiet and still. Dan and I had spent the day there together, and he was putting on his coat to go in to work. His boss had given him the opportunity to work a shift on Christmas Eve at triple pay, and we desperately needed the money, so we decided he should take it. And with Becky's condition being what it was, the night nurse had promised me I wouldn't be bothered if I stayed the night in her room.

Dan turned to me before he left, "Are you sure you're going to be all right? You've never spent the night in the hospital before."

"I'm sure I will," I replied. And then feeling very tired I sighed, "But just once I would like to see one of those angels that Becky always talks about."

As he turned to leave, he kissed me on the cheek and whispered, "I'll be back in the morning."

CHAPTER EIGHT

Beth

$\mathscr{I}$had just fallen asleep and honestly can't tell you if I was dreaming, or whether I awoke beforehand. The one thing I can tell you is that everything that happened that night is as clear in my mind today as it was thirty-four years ago.

The first thing I felt was a soft hand resting gently on my left shoulder, then another hand being placed on my right. I felt a person behind me bend down, put her arms around my shoulders, her head up against mine, and embrace me. She didn't say anything for the longest time; she just held me in a way that reminded me of my mother when I was young.

When she spoke it was not really a whisper, but she said very softly and slowly, almost sobbing, "Oh, Katherine, dear sweet Katherine." She tightened her embrace a little and then repeated the words again.

I had no idea who it was, but it didn't really matter. That

feeling of being loved so completely and unconditionally felt so good and I was so exhausted that, as far as I was concerned, it could have been anyone and I wouldn't have cared.

After a few moments she let go, and with one hand still on my shoulder came around from behind me, turned, and looked directly into my tired, bloodshot eyes. What I saw in front of me was one of the most stunning women I had ever seen. I don't just mean that she was beautiful in the classical sense, which she was. She was simply the most transparently beautiful and angelic person I had ever seen.

She didn't look to be any older than I was, at least not physically, and she had the most penetrating green eyes that seemed to hold some kind of power to see right through my soul. I was sure at first glance that she could see and feel, as if it were on a screen in front of her, every feeling in my heart.

She had auburn hair that flowed softly onto her shoulders, framing her face perfectly and directing my focus back to those heavenly eyes. Her dress was perfectly suited for her look: simple, and elegant, but just stylish enough to be enhancing without drawing one's focus from her countenance. When she spoke to me it was in a kind, gentle voice, but with the authority of a mother.

"Katherine," she insisted softly, "I think it's time we had a talk."

I rubbed my eyes briefly and asked, "I don't mean to be rude, and not that it matters, but who are you?"

"My name is Beth, and I will tell you more about myself in a minute," she replied. "Do you mind if I sit down?" I indicated that of course I didn't mind, but she was already across the room pulling the chair from the other side of Becky's bed over in front of me.

"I understand that you are having a little trouble with who I am and what I am doing here."

That took me back a little, and I just opened my eyes a little wider and replied, "I'm sure I don't know what you are talking about."

"Didn't you tell your husband this evening that just once you'd like to see one of the angels your daughter has been talking about?"

"Yes, I did say that," I admitted, remembering my earlier statement. "But what has it got to do with you, and how did you get in here anyway?"

"I came through the door, the same as you," she replied matter-of-factly. "And like I said before, my name is Beth, and I am the angel you requested."

I nearly slid off of my chair, "Of course you are, and I'm Ladybird Johnson," I replied sarcastically.

"I understand your skepticism," she said quietly, "but whether you believe it or not, that is what I am. I am an angel, and what's more, I am your angel. I have been asked, as a Christmas gift to you, to come here and spend whatever time you need of me and answer any questions that your heart might need answered."

Not understanding exactly what was going on and feeling a little irritated, I snapped, "I don't need any questions answered, but if you're really an angel then maybe you could make my daughter healthy again."

"Dear Katherine," she said, and she sighed as she spoke, "I almost wish I could, but that is one thing that in this case I have no power over. I am simply to answer the questions you have in your heart, and give you whatever comfort I can."

"I knew it," I replied sharply. "Okay, then, if it's answers you have then tell me this: what kind of God and what kind of angels would let a beautiful little girl who would never hurt anyone, suffer like my Becky is doing?"

"My," she gasped. "You sure start with the tough ones, don't you? That's good though. That's one of the most important questions to have answered, and it's probably the best place to start.

"I am going try to help you understand the answer to that question in parts, I hope. So as we discuss different things, I would like you to keep in your mind the part of your question that refers to the nature of God and see if some of the answers don't fall into place. Before we begin, however, do you mind if I ask you a few questions?"

"I guess not," I replied incredulously. "But I thought you were here to answer questions, not ask them."

She went on as if she hadn't heard that last remark. "Katherine, do you think that what is happening to your family has any meaning?"

"None whatsoever," I snapped. "Unless..." and I thought for an instant and then caught myself and repeated, "Absolutely none."

She nodded her head as she watched me answer and then, looking right through me, she asked, "All things being equal, what do you think would be the greatest gift that a parent could give a child?"

"I don't know, love I guess," I responded. "But you keep asking me questions. What is this anyway, a hospital or a classroom?"

"You're partially right about love, but that's a little too simple," she answered directly. And then, as if she had just scored a major point, she went on, "and, incidentally, a classroom is exactly what this is. But try to think in a little more specific terms. Of all that a wise parent could possess and pass on, what would be the one thing he or she might want to leave to their child more than any other?"

By that time I had quit questioning who or what she

was and was occupied trying to think of what exactly she was getting at. Despite all of my efforts to be cynical, I knew within myself that whether she was an angel or not, I liked this woman. I liked her direct approach in speaking to me and, other than feeling as though I was being put on the spot, I liked being challenged to think.

"Let's leave that for now," she said. "We can get back to it." She glanced down briefly, then looked back up directly into my eyes, and taking my hands and holding them firmly between hers, she asked simply and directly, "Katherine, do you think that what is happening to your family is a result of anything that you have done?"

Stunned by the directness of her question, I bowed my head for a moment, bit my lower lip, and then looked up directly into her eyes. With tears welling as I spoke, I simply asked in reply, "Who are you really? And why do you ask me that?" This woman seemed to be familiar with every corner of my soul.

She reached tenderly across to me, and with a handkerchief, wiped the tears from my eyes, brushed my hair back, and said with emphasis, "I know about everything, Katherine. I know where your hurt comes from, and believe me when I tell you that I know exactly how much it hurts."

With that, I began to cry uncontrollably. Between sobs I

spilled my whole heart out to this woman. "Beth, if there is a God, I know He has seen and heard everything I have done and said and that he knows that I have never acknowledged him. If I were Him I would not have anything to do with me; heaven knows I have never had anything to do with Him. I have never wanted, or thought I needed, His help in the past, and I have no right to ask for it now. I just don't understand why—"

She took me in her arms and held me while I continued to cry. Once again I begged, "I don't understand why He would let someone as perfect as my little girl suffer for my weakness."

She held my face between her hands, looked into my eyes, and firmly but lovingly said, "My dear, you are making two major assumptions that you have no right to make."

She wiped a tear from my cheek, brushed my hair back again, and then after a few moments continued, "First, you assume that God is interested only in dealing with us based on what we deserve and gives no consideration to what we need. Secondly, you assume that this life we are living is the only place in time and space that has any meaning.

"Before we go further," she insisted, "it is probably best if you knew a little more about me and about this place. To those of us who belong to the hospital, this is one of the most sacred places on earth. You asked a few minutes ago, maybe sarcastically, if I thought this was a classroom, and in reality that is precisely what it is. To our way of thinking it represents the highest form of learning that God has made available to man. Katherine, there are certain gifts available here and at other places like this, gifts that cannot be obtained anywhere else on earth.

"It is important to know that every angel who serves here at Primary Children's, and there are many of us, actually belongs to the hospital. What I mean by that is that every one of us during our lifetime on earth was either a patient, a volunteer, a part of the medical staff, or a family member of a patient. I happen to have been a patient here during the 1930s when Mamma Rose was the head nurse and the hospital was on North Temple Street. In fact, I was just twelve years old, the same age as Becky, when I graduated from my mortal life.

"Our main function and responsibility is to be of special service to the patients and their families. That service includes lending whatever comfort we can and helping to ensure that every person who comes to Primary Children's has the opportunity to learn and understand all that is possible, so that their time here is not wasted. Occasionally, if the situation calls for it, we are permitted and even encouraged to leave the hospital to fulfill our duties, but most of the time we serve right here within these walls."

CHAPTER NINE

The Classroom

$\mathcal{B}$eth let what she had said sink in a little as she sat there holding my hand and then added, "Katherine, before we continue I need to go back for a moment and clear something up. I know you have honestly felt this way, but maybe you can tell me why you think God would not want to talk to you."

A little sheepishly I replied, "Beth, you know the things I said back when Dan was overseas. They were inexcusable. Not only that, but I have made it a point to prove that I can live my life just fine without God, and I'm sure He knows that. I guess the bottom line is that I don't think the idea of God makes sense."

I paused for a moment to make sure I was going to say the right thing, then continued, "I always thought that for my behavior years ago I may have deserved what I got, but I could never understand why my baby was allowed to die. It certainly wasn't his fault. And Becky getting cancer, I mean, I understand that I had shut God out of my life, but she certainly hadn't. She and Dan have always believed in God, and they pray regularly. That's another thing; what about Dan's heart attack? The only one in the family who is really healthy is me, and I'm the cynic. Now tell me where the logic is in that."

Beth just smiled softly as I rambled. When I had finished she thought for a moment and then answered me with another question. "Katherine, when you referred to what happened years ago and the things you said and did, who do you think you hurt more than anyone?"

"I know it broke Dan's heart," I said sadly.

"And what was his response?"

"After he had been reassured that I still cared for him and needed him, he loved me even more."

"And why do you think he did that?"

I looked away for a moment and then answered, "You know, Beth, for the longest time I asked myself that very question." Suddenly the thought of how distant I had been to him during the past few months made me shudder. "But over the years I have come to believe that, other than Becky, he is the only person I have ever met who truly loves me unconditionally."

Beth looked into my eyes warmly, "My dear, don't you think that just maybe God has the capacity to love you at least that much as well?"

"I guess I've never thought of it that way," was all I could say.

"Katherine, make no mistake about it, the fact that your daughter is here does not mean that anything has been done wrong. Quite the contrary. Those who are brought to Primary Children's are among the finest and most elect of all of God's children. He did not send me here to chastise you; you have done more than enough of that yourself.

"What I was sent to help you understand is that He needs you and what you can give, much more than you can imagine."

"He needs me?" I gasped.

"Does that surprise you?"

"It sure does. But what would He need me for?"

"Katherine, you are a teacher, and a very good one, and you care. You forget, my dear, He knows your heart, not just your words."

Astonished, I simply inquired, "But why all the suffering?"

"I honestly can't answer that for all cases. But go back to my first question for a minute and when you know the answer to that you may understand one possible reason. I'll rephrase the question a little and maybe that will help. If you were a parent who had been down every road, knew every obstacle in that road, had fought every battle and had strengthened your soul through the adversities you had overcome, what more than anything in this world would you desire to leave with your child as a birthright?"

It had been a long time since I had felt that much pure sunlight on my soul, and I began to see where she was going with this. "Putting it that way makes the answer much simpler. I guess that I would want to leave her with the perspective and knowledge that I had gained."

"The knowledge and perspective you had *earned*," she corrected. "And just how would you try to accomplish that?"

I understood clearly by then, and I replied, "There is only one way, isn't there?"

"Yes, Katherine, there is. Not even God would change that. This time of year we celebrate the fact that he sent his Son, who gave His life so that we could be free and have the opportunity to overcome our weaknesses. But even the decision to make His atonement effective in our own lives requires that we accept the challenge and responsibility to learn and grow by *experience*, just as He did."

Beth stood up and walked slowly toward the window, then, turning back she asked, "Katherine, when Becky expressed a desire to learn the violin, where did you send her to study?"

I thought by then I knew where she was leading, so I replied, "Of course we sent her to the best teacher that we could afford."

"And the piano?"

"The same, we sent her to the best in town."

Beth continued the line she was pursuing. "You mean you didn't send her to the easiest teacher?"

"Of course not," I said smiling.

"Or the most convenient?"

"You know I didn't."

"And did Becky ever complain that what was demanded of her by these teachers was too difficult?"

"Many, many times."

"Well, then, why didn't you let her quit and spend the time playing games and watching TV like the other children in the neighborhood?"

"I definitely was tempted a time or two," I admitted, "but it was her decision to pursue those skills, and once the commitment had been made it was my job as a parent, who could see the bigger picture and the benefits of sticking with it, to insist that she follow through."

Beth smiled at me with satisfaction. "Katherine, I think you understand the ways of heaven and nature much more clearly than you'll admit. It has always been the case that one of the hardest truths for humankind to fully embrace is that the most difficult trials are usually reserved for the most noble of God's children."

I nodded to indicate that I had understood her point, but my mind had started to think of another item, so as she paused for a moment I asked, "Beth, I don't mean to change the subject, but there is a question that is bothering me a little. You said that you were only twelve when you died, yet you are a fully grown woman. How can that be?"

She winked at me as if she had planted that question in my mind to help her with the point she was trying to make.

"That's another thing you need to understand. You and I and Becky are all spirits. In fact everyone is a spirit, and as a spirit, each of us, regardless of our physical age, is a fully grown person. What we are trying to do during our time on this earth is teach our physical bodies how to grow to the level that our spirits have already attained.

"That little daughter of yours, lying beside us now, whether you know it or not, is in spirit one of the greatest and most noble women there is. I would guess, based on the priority and importance that Heavenly Father has placed on her care and training, that her soul is of enormous importance to Him."

As I thought back briefly to the events of the past few months, I just smiled softly, nodded, and whispered, "I guess down deep, I've always known that."

"Katherine, when you and I and Becky came to this life, our Father in Heaven really had only one goal in mind for us. Also, when Jesus was born so many Christmases ago, it was for the same purpose, and that purpose and goal was to endow us with the greatest gift that any parent can ever give. He has placed that gift in front of us, but he has camouflaged it behind trials and heartache. All of us will have difficult times, it's just part of the overall package. Whether we then choose to accept the gift that is offered as a result of our trials and experience is completely up to us."

Bit by bit, during my discussion with Beth, I felt my entire soul being filled with light. Right then I felt more at peace than I had ever felt before in my life. I still knew what was ahead and it still hurt, but a subtle and sublime understanding was taking shape in my soul.

Beth went back to the window and looked toward the stars in the southwestern sky. "Katherine, it's nearly time for me to go, but I need to emphasize a couple of things before I do."

She turned back and stood facing me and took my hand again, "Do you feel like some of the questions and doubts in your heart have been answered?"

"Yes, Beth, I really do. And something inside of me tells me that you are correct. God is truly my Heavenly Father, and my heart tells me that he does love me."

"Then, Katherine, this is what I have been asked to tell you. You are as noble and great an individual as I have ever known. Please don't act surprised; somewhere deep inside of yourself, in quiet times when intuition takes over and pushes logic aside, you have always understood that. You were blessed with a truly rare ability to communicate, but that skill needs to be used for the purpose it was intended.

"He needs you, Katherine. But, my dear, and this is the sticky part, He needs *all* of you. Giving a little of yourself won't do; in fact, in your case it might prove more harmful to you than doing nothing at all. If you can get and feel that marvelous gift that you have been given, the only way you can ever hope to keep it is to share it with others. Do everything that your imagination can conceive of in order to accomplish that.

"Katherine, I promise you that as the years go by, even though you may not see her, your daughter will remain with you. In fact, as you give of yourself with everything that you have, your relationship with Becky will continue to grow. As time passes, your memories of her will bring a peace to your soul that you have never known before, and you will never feel closer to her than you will when you are serving others.

Beth had tears in her eyes as she looked at me that last time, "Katherine, as far as I am allowed to understand, this is the only time in your earthly life that we will be able to meet and talk, but I would really like to call you my friend if that's okay with you."

"Of course," I cried, and I stood up and put my arms around her and embraced her tightly.

She then reached inside the pocket of her dress and pulled out a card. "I was told I could give you this note when I finished," she confessed.

I took the card in my hands and turned away to catch the light of the table lamp in the corner to read it. It simply said:

My dear Katherine,

If I could give you just one gift, it would be the gift of understanding, which would include the ability to see the world as God sees it, to feel things as He feels them, and to love as He loves, for when you possess these, you will possess everything.

His Spirit will be with you always, if you will only ask.

Love,

Beth

I turned the card over in my hand and read the other side...

*Who is more worthy to receive God's greatest gift
than a parent who, despite all efforts, watches helplessly
as their child is forced to learn life's most difficult lessons
long before her innocence has passed?*

*And who is more qualified to stand by Christ than a
child, who like him, suffers innocently, while being raised
to the level of the angels?*

"Oh, Beth," I sobbed. "I understand," and I turned
back toward her.

But she was gone.

CHAPTER TEN

"I Love You, Mamma"

For the next few minutes I sat there in the darkness of Becky's room and let the warmth of what had just happened envelop me. Then I simply slid out of my chair onto my knees next to Becky's bed and began to pray. I really don't know how long I spent kneeling there because I don't know exactly how long I had spent talking with Beth. But I had thirty-eight years of catching up to do, so I'm sure it was quite a while.

I was still on my knees as the sunlight broke through the window, and I had just barely returned to the chair when Dan came in.

"Did you get any sleep?" he asked, sounding concerned.

"Not much," I replied softly. "But I feel better inside than I have felt in years." I stood up, looked up into his eyes, put my arms around him, and kissed him like I hadn't done in a long, long time. Suddenly I remembered another time, years before, the day he returned home from

Korea, and I began again to cry. "I love you so much, Dan."

I felt a little hand reach over from the bed and squeeze my hand. When I looked her way I saw Becky looking at me, a weak but impish grin on her face. She just tightened her grip on my hand and winked. Then Dan and I both bent down and gently pulled her into a three-way hug.

"Merry Christmas," she said as loud as she was able.

"Merry Christmas, Sweetheart," Dan said, smiling.

Becky tugged a little at my hand, and I bent down close to her. "Mamma, you met Beth last night, didn't you?" she asked knowingly.

"Yes, Honey, I did, and she was just as nice as you said she was."

"I'm so glad, Mamma. I love you so much."

"I love you too, Sweetheart."

She was visibly tired, and I could see that she was struggling to stay awake long enough to say what she wanted to say. "Mamma, someday I hope Heavenly Father will let me help children here at the hospital just like Beth does."

"You know what," I said quite honestly, "I'm sure you would be terrific at it."

$\mathscr{G}$

Becky woke up only one more time before she died, and that was at nearly midnight on Christmas Day. Dan was sleeping in the chair in the corner on the other side of the room, and I was standing next to her bed holding her hand. She tugged at my hand weakly and a soft smile came across her face. Then, as though she were just drifting off to sleep, without opening her eyes, she said, "I love you, Mamma."

I just stared at that beautiful little face for a long moment, then got up and went over to the chair where Dan was sleeping and woke him. He knew the instant he looked into my eyes what had happened. He put his arms around me, pulled me close to him, and then for the longest time he just sobbed.

I hope I can explain it adequately, but the time we spent with our little girl between when she died and when the hospital staff came in to take care of her became one of the most sacred parts of our lives. There we sat as a family, our chairs pulled close to her bed but still facing each other and each of us holding her hand.

I was first to break the thoughtful silence, "Dan, do you remember the night our son was born?"

"I remember it like it was yesterday," he said softly.

"Well, you told me once that you had a dream that night that helped you deal with it. You've never told me what that dream was and I have never asked. I was just wondering if you would tell me now."

He stood up, slowly walked over to the window, and then turned toward me. "I dreamed that I was sitting in my tent going over the next day's duty roster and a messenger from my platoon came in and announced to me that the company my son was serving in was going to be in our area the following afternoon and that my son wanted to see me while he was there.

"It was odd, I thought at the time, seeing as how I didn't have a son.

"A few minutes later the same messenger came in again and handed me a note. It simply said:

Dad, I have been called back to headquarters unexpectedly and won't be able to see you today. I promise I will see you when I can. I love you, Dad.
                                        Signed,
                                        Private Wilson

"I guess there are a dozen interpretations I could have made, but when I got that letter from you, telling me what had happened, something deep within my heart let me know with absolute certainty what it meant."

He walked back over to where I was sitting, looked down at Becky's little body, brushed his hand tenderly against her cheek, and then looked into my eyes. "Katherine, I really don't believe we ever lost our son. I think we just lost the chance to be with him for a period of time. There is a place in my heart that tells me that he is not a little boy, but a man, and that he is, and forever will be, part of our family. I know it's true because of the peace it brings to my soul when I think of it."

He paused to wipe the tears from his eyes and then said softly, "And somehow I have to feel like Becky has just met him for the first time."

"Oh, Dan," I cried, and I threw my arms around him and buried my head in his chest.

CHAPTER ELEVEN

A Magnificent Obsession

$\mathcal{K}$atherine looked at the faces of the women around her, and each of them was dabbing her eyes with tissues.

"Becky died officially at 12:05 A.M. on December 26, 1966. We had a nice funeral for her three days later, which some of the nurses from the hospital attended. It was so beautiful, and Dorothy arranged for a ladies' quartet to sing 'Scarlet Ribbons.'"

$\mathcal{G}$

That afternoon as Dan and I were walking away from the cemetery, I had my head on his shoulder, and I was sobbing just as I had been all day. From behind me I felt a firm tap on my shoulder, and I turned around to see who it was.

"A short, bright-eyed woman who looked to be in her late forties looked up into my eyes. "Mrs. Wilson, my name is Sarah Madsen. My son David was a friend of Becky's at Primary Children's."

Dan smiled weakly and we both acknowledged her: "You have a handsome little boy," Dan replied.

"He's a handful," she confessed. "He went back into the hospital on Tuesday and had surgery yesterday."

Dan looked kindly at her and asked sincerely, "How did it go?"

"Oh, it went fine, and he's going to be okay, but he made me promise that I would come to Becky's funeral and say hi to her parents. Mr. Wilson, I think he really likes you."

She then looked at me. "Mrs. Wilson..."

"Katherine, you can call me Katherine."

"Thank you." She smiled and handed me a slip of paper with a phone number on it.

"Katherine, we lost David's older sister to leukemia four years ago. She was about the same age as Becky, so I know exactly what you are going through. I won't bother you now, but call me sometime and we can talk."

"Thanks," I said honestly as she took my hand in hers.

❦

I think that Dan and I were still in a daze when we went back to the hospital a couple of days later to get Becky's things. She really didn't have much more than her clothes, and the hospital staff had boxed everything up and had it waiting for us when we got there.

It's really the small things in life that make an impression, you know, and I can still remember how kind and loving everyone was to us that day. We didn't meet a soul who did not call us by name and wish us the best, from the office staff to the nurses on the fifth floor.

It was weeks before I went through that box, and when I did I was heartbroken to find that Becky's candy box was not among her things. Of all the things in this world that I wish I could have found, I think that her box would have been the most precious to me. But even after having the staff go through her room completely two more times, we still couldn't find it.

The next few days passed, and I was sitting in the kitchen by myself about a week or so later, feeling emptier than I had ever felt in my life. I happened to look down briefly, and my eye caught sight of the note Sarah had written, lying by the phone. I kept looking at it every few minutes for about an hour and then feeling like I had nothing to lose, I picked up the phone and dialed.

It sounded like Sarah who answered, so I quickly said, "Is this Sarah?"

"Yes it is, can I help you?"

"Sarah, this is Katherine Wilson. I met you at my daughter's funeral."

"Oh, Katherine, I'm so glad you called. How are you holding up?"

I didn't have the patience to put on airs, and I felt as though she really cared, so I said, "Not too good, Sarah. I'm having a pretty tough day."

"Would you mind if I came over to see you?" she asked immediately.

"No, I wouldn't mind, but how far away do you live?"

She was fidgeting on the other end, looking for a pen as she talked, "You just live on Bryan, don't you, Katherine?"

"Yes, just east of Whittier Elementary."

"Well, I just live up on Kensington, so I could be there in a few minutes. Let me make sure my older daughter is going to be here with David, and I'll come right over."

That began one of the most beautiful friendships I had ever known. Her family was all grown except David, who she said was their little surprise. She and her husband, Melvin, had lived in the same house on Kensington Avenue for twenty-seven years.

Well, that day we just sat there until Dan came home, talking about our little girls and getting to know each other. Before she left, she took me in her arms and hugged me as if she had known me forever. As she held me, she quietly took a book out of her purse and laid it on the coffee table next to us. I glanced down at it. The name of the book was

The Magnificent Obsession by Lloyd C. Douglas.

"Katherine," she said as she put on her coat, "I would like you to go somewhere with me on Monday if you don't mind. We can have lunch first, but I'd like you to come."

"I'd love to," I replied, happy to have somewhere to go.

"Would you do me a favor before I pick you up on Monday then?"

"Sure, what?"

"Would you read that book? It's really important."

"Okay, if you'd like. I'll have it read before you get here on Monday."

So as soon as Dan and I finished supper that night, I began reading. It was a beautiful story, and told of how one man's entire life was changed through service to others and to a cause greater than himself. The more I read, the more I cried, and the more I cried, the more I thought of Beth, and the more I thought of Beth, the more I thought of Becky.

This is exactly what she was talking about, I thought. The change in Robert Merrick's life in the book was exactly what Beth expected of me. And suddenly, as if the lights were just turned on inside my soul, I felt alive again.

Well, Monday came, and Sarah picked me up in her station wagon and took me to her house for lunch. After we had talked awhile she said we needed to be going, so we both got in the car again and she started down Highland Drive.

It was less than five minutes after we got in the car that she turned and asked, "What did you think of the book?"

"It was terrific!'" I gushed. "I cried my eyes out at the end."

"What did you think of what happened to Robert Merrick?"

"Sarah, I'll be honest with you. I think the same thing is happening to me. I just wish I had a little bit of a guide to help me get started."

She looked over at me and winked, "Oh, you do, do you?" She chuckled to herself as she turned onto Vine Street. She drove about two more blocks and then turned into the driveway of a little brick rambler.

Her face turned serious while still retaining its softness. "This is it, Katherine. This is where we get started. This young couple's little four-year-old girl has been diagnosed with a serious heart problem. They are completely heartbroken and desperate, and I think that more than anything else they need a friend."

§

That day was, in every way that matters, the first day of my new life. Sarah introduced me to ways of service that

I never knew existed. The amazing thing was that it never felt like a sacrifice. More than that, it felt invigorating, and the friendships that I developed as a result mean more to me today than all of the money in the world.

It was Sarah who called me in early 1970 and told me that Ruth Flint, a friend of hers on the Women's Endowment Committee, had just explained to her this wonderful idea for a Festival of Trees. Of course I wanted to be a part of it, so I volunteered to serve on a committee. I remember that first year we raised over $47,000, which seemed miraculous. I loved every minute of it, and I was thrilled when they asked me to serve on the Board two years later.

Sarah passed away in 1978 from cancer, and for a time I felt lost. But then Beverly came into the picture along with some other new ladies, and suddenly I was a senior member with a whole new set of responsibilities.

I don't want you think that I haven't missed Becky. A day hasn't gone by that I don't think of her. But there is a world of difference between hurting over the loss of someone and feeling despair, and never do I feel as close to her as when I am doing something on behalf of the hospital."

ॐ

The ladies in the room could see that Katherine was nearly out of energy as she struggled to finish. She began to put her scarf around her neck and nodded to Beverly as she continued.

"Well, Dan and I had twenty-two more years together before he passed away, and though through most of them his health was not good, they were wonderful years all the same."

Then, as if the battery within her had all but run down, she announced, "Well, ladies, that's my story. I hope you understand why I had to tell you all about it now."

One by one each of the women in the room came over to her and, with tears in their eyes, embraced her. Beverly then helped her on with her coat, and as she pulled it around her, Katherine turned and said, "Thank you for everything. I love you all."

CHAPTER TWELVE

The Angel of Eleventh Avenue

$\mathcal{I}$t was nearly four weeks later. Snow was falling steadily, and the streetlights were just coming on as Beverly turned down the lane and into her driveway. She parked the car in the garage and entered the house through the kitchen just as the phone rang. She quickly put her handbag on the counter and lifted the receiver.

A somber female voice came on as she picked it up. "Beverly, this is Dorothy. I'm sorry to bother you on Christmas Eve, but I've been trying to get hold of you all afternoon. Katherine's doctor called me late this morning to tell me that he doesn't think she will make it through the night. I'm over here at the hospital now, and I promised Katherine I would call you if the time got close."

Beverly responded warmly, "Oh, I'm so glad you did. I've already told Rex and the kids that I may have to be gone for a while this evening, and they are prepared for it. So if you'll give me about twenty minutes or so, I'll be right there."

A million different thoughts were going through Beverly's mind as she drove down the beltway, got off on Foothill Drive, and then made her way up to the Huntsman Cancer Institute. One part of her was profoundly sad, but the other part was surprisingly joyous. All she could think about was how at peace Katherine was about everything and how much she was looking forward to what was to come.

I hope when my time comes I can understand and feel what she feels, she thought to herself.

After she had parked her car and taken the elevator to the floor where Katherine's room was, she ran into Emily Thompson in the hall.

"I'm so glad you got here," Emily said as she gave her a warm hug.

When they opened the door to Katherine's room, they found Dorothy sitting in the chair next to the bed and Katherine fast asleep. In their greetings, the two women almost didn't notice the small Christmas tree on the table in the corner of the room. After a time, they looked over at the little tree and then turned in surprise and looked at each other.

"Isn't that...?" Emily gasped.

"That's the Scarlet Ribbons tree from the festival!" Beverly interrupted excitedly. "How did that get here?"

Dorothy answered, "A woman brought it in earlier today. She said she had bought it at the festival and had seen

Katherine stop to admire it. She also left the presents that came with it as well. Apparently at least one of them is a real gift because she marked it and said to make sure Katherine opened it as soon as she was awake. I have just been waiting and hoping she'll open her eyes so I can show it to her."

Beverly and Emily both walked over to the table in the corner and examined the little tree.

"This is perfect," Emily mused as she ran the ribbons of one of the velvet bows through her fingers.

Beverly picked up the present that had Katherine's name on it and gently placed it on the bed next to her. "I wonder what's in the gift?" she thought out loud.

Dorothy motioned for them to follow her into the hallway, leaving the door slightly ajar as they walked down the hall to the nurse's station. They listened together as the nurse on duty brought them up to the minute as to what Katherine's condition had been that day.

"She has moments," the nurse said, "but as weak as she's been she could go at any time." She motioned to the monitor behind the counter, which indicated Katherine's heart rate, and then continued with what she was saying.

They had been talking with the nurse for five or ten minutes when they noticed that the monitor suddenly showed that the heart rate had risen dramatically and then suddenly there was none.

Together they hurried back down the hall to Katherine's room. They got to where the door was ajar, but before they could push it open they stopped in their tracks. Their eyes grew wide in disbelief, and Emily put her hand over her mouth and gasped at what the three of them saw.

Through the opening they could see Katherine, lying motionless, with her eyes closed and the most beautiful and peaceful smile on her face. In her hands she held the gift from under the tree, which Beverly had placed on the bed next to her. It had been opened and the paper was lying on the floor.

What they saw in her hands was an old white See's Candy box with the corners tattered and the lid pulled off. The box was tipped slightly so that they could see the contents, and within the box was a paper doll with her clothes, a half a dozen or so faded red ribbons, and a 45 RPM record of the song "Scarlet Ribbons." To the side of Katherine's bed, with her back to the door and apparently unaware that anyone was watching, stood the woman who had sung the song at the festival. Tenderly, she pushed back the hair from Katherine's forehead, bent down, kissed her gently, and whispered,

"I love you, Mamma..."

About the Author

The late Roy Bates had been a patient at Primary Children's Hospital as a child, and he wrote *The Angel of Eleventh Avenue* to give something back to the place that restored and encouraged him. He lived in Salt Lake City, Utah, and is survived by his wife and six children.